GETTING TO KNOW
THE U.S. PRESIDENTS

W A R R E N   G.
HARDING

TWENTY-NINTH PRESIDENT
1921 – 1923

WRITTEN AND ILLUSTRATED BY MIKE VENEZIA

CHILDREN'S PRESS®
A DIVISION OF SCHOLASTIC INC.
NEW YORK   TORONTO   LONDON   AUCKLAND   SYDNEY
MEXICO CITY   NEW DELHI   HONG KONG
DANBURY, CONNECTICUT

Reading Consultant: Nanci R. Vargus, Ed.D., Assistant Professor, School of Education, University of Indianapolis

Historical Consultant: Marc J. Selverstone, Ph.D., Assistant Professor, Miller Center of Public Affairs, University of Virginia

Photographs © 2007: Art Resource, NY: 3 (National Portrait Gallery, Smithsonian Institution, Washington, DC); Bridgeman Art Library International Ltd., London/New York: 26 (New-York Historical Society, New York); Corbis Images: 6, 20, 24, 25, 29, 30, 31 (Bettmann), 11 (Layne Kennedy), 11 inset, 13, 22, 32; Library of Congress: 14, 17; The Image Works/Roger-Viollet/Topham: 23 center.

Colorist for illustrations: Andrew Day

Library of Congress Cataloging-in-Publication Data

Venezia, Mike.
  Warren G. Harding / written and illustrated by Mike Venezia.
      p. cm. — (Getting to know the U.S. presidents)
  ISBN 10: 0-516-22633-9 (lib. bdg.)   0-516-25228-3 (pbk.)
  ISBN 13: 978-0-516-22633-0 (lib. bdg.)   978-0-516-25228-5 (pbk.)
  1. Harding, Warren G. (Warren Gamaliel), 1865-1923—Juvenile literature. 2. Presidents—United States—Biography—Juvenile literature. I. Title.
  E786.V46 2007
  973.91'4092-dc22

                                        2006000455

1 2 3 4 5 6 7 8 9 10 R 16 15 14 13 12 11 10 09 08 07

A portrait of President Warren G. Harding by Margaret Lindsey Williams (National Portrait Gallery, Smithsonian Institution, Washington, D.C.)

Warren G. Harding was born in 1865 in Blooming Grove, Ohio. He became the twenty-ninth president of the United States in 1921. Even though President Harding did some good things during his term, many historians consider him to have been the worst of all presidents.

One of President Harding's biggest problems was that he was such a friendly, fun-loving person. He wanted his friends to be happy and often gave them important government jobs. Some of these friends tricked President Harding. They turned out to be sneaky and took government money for themselves.

President Harding either didn't know his friends were crooks or didn't care. He liked to play poker, drink whiskey, chew tobacco, tell jokes, and stay up late with his buddies. Once, the president gambled away an entire set of expensive White House dishes in a card game!

Six-year-old Warren Harding (center) with his sisters

As a young boy, Warren G. Harding kept busy with all kinds of farm chores. He enjoyed playing with his younger brother and sisters in the woods and fields near his home. Warren attended a one-room schoolhouse, where he learned to read, write, and spell.

Warren was a pretty normal boy, but his father, George Tryon Harding, was unusual in many ways. Mr. Harding could never make up his mind about what he wanted to be.

First he tried being a farmer. Then he was a teacher. He thought about becoming a veterinarian, but then decided to become a doctor. What he spent most of his time doing was swapping things. George Harding loved to make deals. He would trade anything he had to get something he didn't have.

When Warren was about ten years old, his father made two deals that Warren thought were great. First, Mr. Harding got a cornet, which he gave to his son. A cornet is similar to a trumpet. Warren loved the instrument and learned to play it well. Next, Mr. Harding bought a small newspaper business. It turned out to be an excellent place for Warren to work. The previous owner taught Warren everything he needed to know about running a newspaper, including setting type and working the presses.

Warren G. Harding loved the newspaper business. When he went away to Ohio Central College, he and a friend ran a college newspaper. For some reason, after he graduated, Warren didn't look for a newspaper job right away. First he taught at a small country school. But Warren didn't care for the rowdy students and quit after the first semester.

As a young man, Warren settled in Marion, Ohio, where he ran a small newspaper. He lived in this house in Marion for many years.

Warren then moved to Marion, Ohio, where his parents lived. He studied law for a while, then tried being an insurance salesman. Finally, Warren decided to get back into the newspaper business. In 1884, Warren was able to borrow enough money to buy a small paper called the *Marion Star*.

Warren worked as hard as he could as an editor and publisher. He made friends all over Marion, Ohio, while collecting stories for his paper. Warren was such a good-natured reporter that people liked and trusted him. He would never print a story that was mean or would hurt someone's feelings.

The offices of the *Marion Star*, Harding's newspaper

Many of the stories the *Marion Star* printed were about politics and the Ohio state government. There were two main political organizations in Ohio at the time, the Republican Party and the Democratic Party. Even though Warren favored the Republicans, his stories were always fair to each side.

Florence Harding

The friendly, handsome, and fun-loving Warren attracted lots of girlfriends. One of them was Florence "Flossie" DeWolf. Flossie was five years older than Warren. She came from a very wealthy family and was crazy about Warren. Flossie chased him around and wouldn't leave him alone until he agreed to marry her.

In 1891, Warren and Flossie were married. Flossie turned out to be an excellent businesswoman. With her help, the *Marion Star* became a really successful newspaper. Flossie took care of the office work. This gave Warren more time to gather and write interesting stories.

Workers at the *Marion Star* loved their jobs. Warren shared profits with his employees, and never fired even one of them. Warren had friends all over Marion. He joined local clubs and organizations, and played in the town's band too.

Warren G. Harding as a U.S. senator

Soon many people in Marion thought Warren should run for political office. Warren agreed. In 1899, Warren G. Harding ran for and won two terms in the Ohio state senate. Later, he was elected lieutenant governor of Ohio. A few years after that, Warren was elected a U.S. senator. In 1915, Warren and Flossie moved to Washington, D.C.

Warren wasn't the busiest senator, though. He actually missed more Senate meetings than he attended. It seemed like Senator Harding skipped meetings in which major disagreements or arguments might come up. When he did show up, Warren avoided giving his opinion on touchy subjects. He would do almost anything to keep from making enemies.

Warren's plan worked. He never offended anyone and was well liked by both Republicans and Democrats in Washington, D.C. It was at this time that Warren started getting to know some dishonest men. Warren loved playing golf and cards with them. Some of these friends would later end up stealing money from the government and embarrassing the United States.

The 1920 Republican National Convention in Chicago, Illinois

In 1920, Warren G. Harding attended the Republican National Convention in Chicago. Political conventions are huge meeting places where party members choose a candidate to run for president in the next election. No one ever thought Warren G. Harding would be nominated, but during the convention he suddenly seemed like a great choice. Warren was friends with everyone, he was a successful businessman, and he looked like a president. The Republican Party decided Warren would be their man.

World War I soldiers in battle

When Warren G. Harding was running for president, the United States was just getting over a terrible war. Millions of soldiers and innocent people had lost their lives during World War I. Most of the fighting took place in Europe. When American soldiers returned home, people were relieved. They wanted to forget about war and get back to their normal lives.

Warren G. Harding knew how people felt, and said he would return the United States to normalcy. He won the 1920 election by a huge number of votes. People liked his hopeful message. The election of 1920 was also the first one in which women from every state could finally vote. Some of Warren's supporters believed that women voted for Warren because he was so handsome.

President Harding (fourth from left) getting ready to go fishing with his friends

One of President Harding's first tasks was to choose his cabinet members and advisors. Harding wanted the best men in the country to help him run the United States.

Some cabinet members truly were the best men for the job. Some, however, turned out to be liars and thieves who cared only about themselves. President Harding spent as much time as he could with his advisors, working or sometimes just having fun.

President Harding playing golf in Palm Beach, Florida

A magazine cover showing people partying during the Roaring Twenties

Warren G. Harding was president during the period known as the Roaring Twenties. It was also called the Jazz Age. Drinking alcoholic beverages was against the law at the time. Secret illegal bars, called speakeasies, opened up all over the country. It was popular for men and women to stay out late, dancing and partying. It seemed like people wanted to forget the serious problems of the past and have one long party.

President Harding and his wife did their part to help cheer up the nation. They opened up the White House to visitors and tourists. It was a nice change from the gloomy mood of the war years. Sometimes Flossie guided groups of tourists herself.

President Harding started out doing a pretty good job. He helped establish the Bureau of the Budget. This department kept track of the amount of money the government spent each year. He got England and Japan to go along with the United States to reduce the size of their navies.

President Harding signing a bill into law

Reducing weapons and warships was an important step toward world peace. Once, President Harding was brave enough to lecture a huge southern crowd about their unfair treatment of African Americans.

Things didn't go well for long, though. Near the end of his second year in office, President Harding learned about some dishonest activities his cabinet members and advisors were involved in.

In what became known as the Teapot Dome Scandal, U.S. Secretary of the Interior Albert Fall (left) made money by secretly leasing government land to the oil company of his friend Harry Sinclair (right).

One close advisor was caught selling military supplies and keeping the money for himself. A cabinet member, Albert Fall, allowed oil companies to drill for oil in a government-owned area in Wyoming called Teapot Dome. The oilmen had no right to do this. They paid Albert Fall lots of money to

This political cartoon pokes fun at how the U.S. government was clouded by the Teapot Dome Scandal in 1923.

get their way. Embarrassing and illegal situations like this are called scandals.

In 1923, President Harding decided to take a train tour across the country. He wanted to let everyone know that everything was all right, and that the scandals they may have heard about were under control.

President Harding
and his wife during
his last train tour

Sadly, on August 2, 1923, during a stop on his tour, President Harding died of a heart attack. The nation was shocked. The president was only fifty-seven years old.

Unfortunately, many of the good things President Harding had done were soon forgotten. Instead, people remembered the embarrassing scandals. Even though Warren G. Harding had nothing to do with the dishonest dealings of his friends, he was severely criticized. President Harding was blamed for not having the wisdom or leadership skill to avoid putting corrupt people in powerful positions.